What Word?

Graded Cloze Texts and Comprehension Exercises

Lynn Hutchinson

HODDER AND STOUGHTON
LONDON SYDNEY AUCKLAND TORONTO

British Library Cataloguing in Publication Data

Hutchison, Lynn
    What word?: graded cloze texts and comprehension
    exercises.
    1. Cloze procedure
    I. Title
    428.4'076   LB1050.3

    ISBN 0-340-37687-2

Printed in Great Britain for Hodder and Stoughton Educational,
a division of Hodder and Stoughton Ltd,
Mill Road, Dunton Green, Sevenoaks, Kent
by Butler & Tanner Ltd, Frome, Somerset

Contents

An introduction and a key to the cloze texts are available free on application. Please write, enclosing a large stamped addressed envelope, to **The Primary Editorial Department, Hodder and Stoughton Educational, PO Box 702, Dunton Green, Sevenoaks, Kent, TN13 2YD.**

The Angler

The angler jumped to his feet. He had a catch! Danny could hardly see the ____. It was stretched tight now. It jerked ____ side to side. The fish was trying to get ____.

Slowly the angler reeled in the line. Slowly he ____ the fish nearer. The line stopped jerking. Danny thought the ____ was getting tired. The man pulled it ____ a landing net. Then he lifted it out of the ____.

Danny saw the fish flop weakly. The ____ bent over it. He tried to remove the ____. It was caught deep in the ____. At last he pulled it out. Danny ____ him lift the fish. In a moment it was ____ in the pond.

Now answer these questions in sentences:

1. Why does the line go tight?
2. Why do you think the fish is brought in slowly?
3. How does Danny know the fish is tired?
4. What is the net for?
5. Why do you think the hook is taken out?
6. Why do you think the fish is put back?

On the Boat

Laura looked in the cabin. It was a very small room. It only ____ three sides.

'Is this ____ I'll sleep?'

'Yes,' said her mother. 'Joe ____ sleep in the other berth.'

The cabin ____ in the bows of the ____. There were bunks on two sides. Over ____ were high, narrow windows. Laura ____ up. Now she could see the river. Her ____ made up the berths.

Later, ____ lay in her berth. ____ was asleep. The boat rocked. She rocked ____ the boat. The movement kept her ____. The water sloshed. Would she ever ____ to sleep?

Her next thought was 'Where ____ I?' She opened her eyes. Sunlight ____ through the high window.

Now answer these questions in sentences:

1. What did the cabin look like?
2. Why was it such a funny shape?
3. Who do you think Joe was?
4. What do you think a berth is?
5. What is strange about going to bed on a boat?
6. What can you tell about Laura's first sleep on the boat?

Off the Bike

Roger cycled down the road. From the handle-bars ____ his bag. Rain pattered down. Roger speeded ____ . He was nearly home.

The ____ swung into the wheel. The wheel jerked ____ one side. Roger lost his balance. His hands ____ their grip. He felt himself flying ____ the air.

Then the ground hit him. ____ was cold. He couldn't move. The breath had left ____ body. He tried to rise. ____ happened. Then he felt hands lifting ____ . He knew he shouldn't be moved. He ____ have broken his back. He ____ to say 'no', but no voice came.

____ was lucky. No bones were ____ . His face was stitched. He was ____ bruised. He got better. Then he ____ panniers for his bike.

Now answer these questions in sentences:

1. Why does Roger cycle quickly?
2. What causes the accident?
3. How does Roger feel when he hits the ground?
4. Why shouldn't Roger be moved?
5. Why can't Roger say 'no'?
6. Why do you think Roger bought panniers?

The Spider

Tom heard a scream. He ran upstairs. His mother stood, white-faced.

'____ the matter, Mum?'

'Look over there!'

Tom ____ where she was pointing. On the wall ____ a spider. It wasn't small. ____ the other hand it wasn't huge. ____ was just quite big.

'Tom, could ____ move it?' His mother's voice shook.

'Why?' ____ Tom. 'It won't hurt you!'

'Please, just ____ it away.'

Tom was puzzled. There was ____ to be afraid of. Spiders couldn't ____ humans. Not in this country, anyway. ____ was his mother frightened of?

'I ____ help it, Tom. I won't ____ until it's out of the house.'

Tom scooped it ____ in his hands. He took it downstairs. He ____ it scuttle down the path.

Now answer these questions in sentences:

1. How does Tom know he's needed?
2. What has upset his mother?
3. Why is she upset?
4. How does Tom feel about spiders?
5. What does Tom do to the spider?
6. Are you more like Tom or his mother? Why?

Not as Bad as it Looks

A man called, 'What's it like?'

'Not as bad ____ it looks!' came the reply.

Claire wasn't sure. There ____ no children on this ride. ____ hoped she might seem too young!

'It's ____ turn!' said Tina.

Claire followed Tina to ____ seat. All the seats ____ to revolve. They spun faster and ____. The seats swung out ____ people's heads.

The whole ride tipped up! Now ____ spun on its side. Claire didn't mind ____ up. She hated swooping down. She felt as ____ she was being dashed to the ground. Then she ____ swept into the air again! She felt ____.

'It's not as bad as it ____!' shouted Tina.

'It's a hundred times ____,' moaned Claire.

Now answer these questions in sentences:

1. What are Tina and Claire riding on?
2. Where do you think they are?
3. What is special about this ride?
4. What sort of girl is Tina?
5. What sort of girl is Claire?
6. Why does Claire not agree with Tina at the end?

The Show

Come to the show! See Felix the fire-eater! See the smallest clown ____ the world! Watch the Master ____ Magic!

Stuart listened. Could he ____ to go? He counted the money in ____ pocket. He bought a ticket. He ____ into the tent.

Inside were ____ of planks. They were arranged ____ tiers. He chose a high seat.

Stuart laughed ____ the clown's car fell apart. The ____ amazed him. He rolled burning sticks ____ his body. He put out ____ in his mouth. He even blew flames!

The ____ of Magic made doves appear. The best trick was ____ he blew up a balloon. Then he ____ a gun at it. It popped. ____ flew a dove!

Stuart went home. He ____ wait to tell his sister ____ it!

Now answer these questions in sentences:

1. What does Stuart go to see?
2. Why does Stuart choose a high seat?
3. Which act did Stuart find amazing?
4. Which magic trick did Stuart like best?
5. What do you know about Stuart's sister?
6. Which of these acts would you most like to see and why?

Tornado

The storm raged. Over the noise came a bang. Then ____ were crashes.

'What was that?' ____ Robert. His father, alarmed, ____ to the window. Robert followed. ____ couldn't believe his eyes. Parts ____ the garden shed blew past. Looking up, Robert ____ a dustbin. It passed by ____ ceiling height. Slapping noises ____ from next door's roof. The slates ____ flapping up and down. Then ____ were torn off. They were swirled round ____ the air. Then they fell ____ hailstones.

Robert looked up. Between the clouds the sky ____ a dark yellow. He could see a dark whirling funnel. ____ reached down from one black cloud. It was ____ down the estate. Sheds and hutches were ____ to pieces. The wreckage fell all ____ .

'A tornado!' whispered Robert.

Now answer these questions in sentences:

1. What do you think made the bang and crashing noises?
2. What does Robert see that he finds hard to believe?
3. Why do the slates flap up and down?
4. What do you think happens to what is in the sheds and hutches?
5. What does the tornado look like?
6. What does the tornado do?

The Fox Cubs

The fox cubs stared at Anna. Anna _____ back. They weren't frightened. But they _____ friendly either. The cubs lost interest first. _____ went back to their games. _____ watched. They bounded round their run. They dodged _____ bales of straw. They ran up _____ trunks.

'They are very playful,' Anna _____. 'Are they tame?'

Mr Bentley sighed. '_____, and that's the problem. They aren't wild _____ they aren't tame. They are losing some _____ their wild instincts. But they will never _____ pets.'

'Will you keep _____ like this?' Anna asked.

'I could. It _____ be prison for all their _____.'

'What will you do?'

'I _____ know yet,' said Mr Bentley. 'Should _____ let loose two killers? Could they survive? Or _____ I shoot them now? What do _____ think?'

Now answer these questions in sentences:

1. Where are the fox cubs?
2. What do the fox cubs do which a wild fox wouldn't do?
3. Why doesn't Mr Bentley want to keep the foxes as they are?
4. What does Mr Bentley mean about letting loose two killers?
5. Why does he think they might not survive?
6. What would you do?

Down River

Lynda's parents and sister stood on the deck of the cruiser. They watched _____ row down river. Soon she _____ at the bend in the _____.

'That's far enough!' they _____.

They saw Lynda _____ the boat round. Then _____ watched her start to row towards _____. She rowed and rowed.

'She's _____ getting here very fast!' _____ Susan.

Her father said, 'She's not _____ headway at all. I _____ what the problem is! _____ the ebb tide! This _____ a tidal river. The tide is _____ out!'

'Susan, run along the _____. See if you can help her _____ the boat to the side,' said their mother.

'I'll get _____ to turn this boat round,' their _____ said.

Now answer these questions in sentences:

1. In which direction does Lynda row?
2. Why does Lynda have trouble in rowing back?
3. What effect does the ebb tide have on the river?
4. Why does the mother suggest Susan should help Lynda bring the boat to the side?
5. What can you tell about Susan?
6. What does their father intend to do?

First Day

It was Darren's first day ___ school. He felt very grown-up now, ___ his new clothes.

He went ___ the school. He put his school bag ___ the radiator. Then he ___ up his jacket. Just then, a plimsoll ___ out. It went down the back ___ the radiator. It didn't ___ to the floor. It got stuck half way ___. Darren slipped his arm behind to ___ it. He touched the plimsoll. Then he ___ his arm was stuck.

His friends ___ to get him out. Then the teacher tried, and the head. ___ the end they phoned the fire brigade. They ___ to cut the pipe to get Darren's ___ out. As they did, water spurted all ___ the floor.

No one ___ ever forget Darren's first day at ___!

Now answer these questions in sentences:

1. Why does Darren feel very grown-up?
2. Why do you think Darren put his bag on the radiator?
3. Why did Darren put his arm behind the radiator?
4. Why was the fire brigade called?
5. What did the fire brigade have to do to get Darren's arm out?
6. How did the floor get wet?

Last Secret

Captain Benson moaned. He tossed his head from ____ to side.

'He'll not last much ____,' the first mate whispered. The bosun spoke.

'Cap'n, ____ you hear me? It's time to ____ your mind at rest. You need to make ____ peace now.'

The Captain roared, 'You vultures! I'm ____ telling you where the treasure ____! I'll live through this. If I ____ you, you'd cut my throat!' ____ started coughing. Then he fell back. ____ eyes closed.

'No, no,' the bosun ____. 'You're our Captain! But you're dying. You ____ see the gold and silver again. It's no ____ to you now. Better tell ____ where it is. I'll stop it getting ____ the wrong hands.'

The mate said, 'You're ____ your breath. He's just died.'

Now answer these questions in sentences:

1. What is Captain Benson's secret?
2. What does the Bosun want to know?
3. How does the bosun try to persuade the Captain to tell him the secret?
4. Why does the Captain think the others would cut his throat?
5. Why does the Captain call the men 'vultures'?
6. What sort of people are these?

Bats

Summer is the batty time of year! It is ____ a mother bat finds a dark place. There she ____ have her baby. She sometimes chooses the loft ____ a house. She will go there ____ other bats. They will form a colony.

____ people worry about them coming out ____ night. They fear the bats will drink ____ blood! This is just a story. They ____ never been caught so far! ____ prefer insects.

Bats are not pests. They ____ chew wires. They don't gnaw wood. Squirrels do ____ they get into a loft. A lot of ____ don't like bats. They ____ cuddly.

Bat-lovers say, 'Don't panic! They will ____ on their own. It will ____ in August. That is when the ____ are old enough.'

Now answer these questions in sentences:

1. At what time of year are bats not a problem in houses?
2. How many babies does a bat have at a time?
3. Why do mother bats like lofts?
4. What is a colony?
5. What do squirrels do in lofts?
6. Why do people not like bats?

Birthday Wish

'I wish I had a dog,' Matthew said. It ____ have been the hundredth time ____ week. His parents sighed.

'You know ____ well why you haven't,' his father ____. 'There's no one home all day. It's ____ fair to keep a dog shut ____ all day.'

'We could ____ it in the garden. It could ____ round,' Matthew argued.

'It would ____ be lonely. Lonely dogs bark, and ____. They also get up to ____. No, Matthew, you can't have a ____.'

Matthew still hoped. It was his ____ soon. His parents ____ most likely trying to stop him ____ guessing. They did that last year ____ his bike. They said he was ____ young. Then on his birthday there ____ his racer.

The night ____ Matthew could hardly sleep.

The watch was a very ____ one.

Now answer these questions in sentences:

1. Why do Matthew's parents sigh?
2. Why would a dog be lonely?
3. Can you guess what Matthew's mother does in the day?
4. What had Matthew's parents said about a racing bike last year?
5. Why does Matthew think he might still get a dog even though his parents say no?
6. What did Matthew's parents give him for his birthday?

Saved

The engine noise sounded muffled in the mist.

'How will you know ____ the land is?' I asked.

'We'll ____ to guess,' was the reply. One ____ the sailors peered into the ____.

'That way, I think!' he ____. The other sailor moved the tiller. The ____ changed course.

Without warning, a large shape broke the surface of the ____. It dived again quickly. More ____ followed.

'Dolphins!' breathed one of the sailors. 'They ____ pushing us round!'

Indeed, the ____ had changed its course. The movements of the ____ had forced it round. The sailors steered along the new ____. We looked back. The mist shifted ____ a moment. We saw high, jagged rocks. Then the mist ____ down again.

Now answer these questions in sentences:

1. What problems are the people in this boat having?
2. What sort of boat do you think these people are in?
3. What effect do the dolphins have?
4. What do the people see through the gap in the mist?
5. What would have happened if it hadn't been for the dolphins?
6. Why do you think the dolphins do what they do?

The Deer

Simon and his ___ were driving to the station. It ___ early evening. The narrow road twisted ___ went into the woods. At each ___ were banks and high fences. A car approached. Without ___ a deer came leaping over the fence ___ the other side of the road. It ___ in front of the car coming towards ___. Then it ran in ___ of theirs. Simon's father braked hard. There was a screech of ___, then a thud.

Simon and ___ father scrambled out of the car. The ___ was trying to get ___. It was dragging its back ___ behind it. It was terrified. Yet it never ___ a sound.

'What shall we ___?' Simon cried.

'We'll ___ down to the station and ___ the police. They will send someone ___.'

Now answer these questions in sentences:

1. What sort of place is it where the accident happened?
2. What do you think the deer was trying to do?
3. Which car did the deer run in front of first?
4. Why do you think Simon's father didn't swerve?
5. Why did the deer try to get away?
6. What do you think the police would do?

Pea Picking

My Mum picked peas when she was a ____. Children picked the pods off long rows. ____ said it took ages. She ____ paid by the bucket. Women and ____ did it to earn extra money. There was a lot of ____ on the land in the summer. ____ Mum said pea picking was slave labour.

My brother ____ on a farm. He drives a machine ____ harvests the peas. It is shared ____ ten farmers. That is because it ____ so much. It was over £120,000. It is kept busy ____ June onwards. The peas are grown ____ 500 acres of land. Over a thousand tons of ____ are sold each year. The machine ____ them all. It picks them and shells ____. Then they are chilled to ____ them fresh.

Now answer these questions in sentences:

1. Why did the mother pick peas?
2. Why was it a slow job?
3. Why do you think the mother called it slave labour?
4. Why used there to be a lot of work on the land in summer?
5. How much do you think each farmer would pay towards the pea harvester?
6. Who do you think buys all these peas, and what for?

Dead Man's Fingers

Patrick and John were camping.

The first night ____ fine. They had an early breakfast. Then ____ had a late breakfast. ____ lunch-time they ate ____ last tin.

'We'll have to find ____ own tea,' Patrick said. He found ____ blackberries. John found some unripe hazel ____. It wasn't enough.

John found a plant ____ looked like a carrot. He dug ____ up. Underneath it ____ like a parsnip. He washed it and bit a ____ off.

'This is nice,' he ____.

They cooked some roots for ____. Soon after, Patrick was sick ____ couldn't stand up. John, who'd eaten ____, went for help. They were both ____ to hospital.

'Never do that again!' ____ were told. 'You've eaten a plant ____ Dead Man's Fingers. You could both have ____.'

Now answer these questions in sentences:

1. Why did Patrick and John have two breakfasts?
2. Why did the boys have to find their own tea?
3. What was the plant which John found like?
4. What effect did the plant have?
5. Why do you think the plant was called Dead Man's Fingers?
6. What lesson do you think the boys have learned?

At the Bank

Kim hurried to work. She wondered ____ Martin would have opened up yet. The bank was ____ the next corner. She ran ____ the steps and pushed the heavy ____. As it started to open ____ glimpsed Martin. With horror she ____ him pulled backwards through the inner door. ____ arm was round his throat.

____ turned and ran. She hoped she ____ been seen. The police station was 300 metres up the ____. She burst through the doors ____, 'There's a robbery! At the bank! They've got Martin!' She ____ if they would believe her.

They ____. But Kim had been seen. ____ the time the police arrived the thieves had ____ off. Martin was shaken ____ unhurt. The police made a thorough search. They ____ only an open skylight.

Now answer these questions in sentences:

1. Who was at work first?
2. How do you think the thieves got in?
3. Why didn't Kim phone 999?
4. Why do you think she thought the police might not believe her?
5. Why did the man run away?
6. What do you think the robbers' plan was?

Owen's Dream

The gang crept into the house. It ____ been empty for a long time. People ____ it was haunted. They didn't ____ any ghosts. They ____ find rotting wood and boards ____ creaked. Owen went upstairs to ____. He found only sagging floors, empty ____, and cobwebs.

Martin moved the plank from the window. They ____ back through the gap, and ____ the plank back.

That night, Owen dreamt ____ the house. He dreamt that he went ____. On the landing he stumbled, and fell ____ the banister. It broke, and he started to fall. He woke ____ a start.

The next day, the ____ went back to the house. Owen climbed the ____. He gave the banister a ____. It broke.

Now answer these questions in sentences:

1. Why do you think the gang went into the house?
2. How did they get in?
3. What can you tell about the condition of the house?
4. What makes Owen wake up?
5. Why did Owen go upstairs again on the second day?
6. How do you explain Owen's dream?

Big Babies

Human beings are mammals. Dogs, mice and lions ____ mammals. Mammals are creatures ____ have warm blood. They have backbones. They also ____ live babies which need their mother's milk ____ first. They don't hatch ____ of eggs, and they can't ____ adult food straight away.

There are many mammals in the world. The ____ are the whales. Their babies ____ milk to grow, just ____ human babies. Baby sperm whales need lots of ____. They are bigger ____ a sitting-room when they are ____! They grow fast. They need 100 kilos of milk ____ day. Their weight increases by five kilos ____ hour! That is 120 kilos in a day. ____ double their length in a year. ____ about four years old they are ____ grown.

Now answer these questions in sentences:

1. How are dogs and whales the same?
2. What have mammals got in common?
3. What must a baby mammal have when it is born?
4. Which mammals have the biggest babies?
5. Are chickens mammals?
6. When is a whale old enough to have babies of its own?

The Photo

'Who is that with the horse?' I _____. I pointed to a photo _____ a young man with a _____ and cart.

'That was _____ brother, Jack,' my great aunt _____. 'He was a carter.' She sighed. 'He _____ came back from the war. We never _____ the horse again, either.'

I wanted to _____ what had happened to the _____.

'All the horses _____ the village were taken away. _____ were needed in the war. One _____ some men came. They took _____ all. Some _____ tried to hide _____ horses, but they were found out. The horses were _____ in pairs to a long rope. We _____ known those horses most of _____ lives. It was like seeing our friends _____. In those days we _____ on horses for farming and transport. _____ were lost without them.'

Now answer these questions in sentences:

1. What do you think had happened to Jack?
2. For what reason were the horses taken away?
3. Which war do you think this was?
4. In what ways were the horses like friends?
5. Why did some people try to hide their horses?
6. How do you think the villagers managed when the horses went?

Lassie

'What is the matter ＿＿ that dog?' asked Mr Coe. 'She's ＿＿ up and down all evening!'

Lassie ＿＿ on the prowl again. She padded ＿＿ the room. She sniffed the air. ＿＿ made little whimpers in her ＿＿.

'Do you think she is ＿＿?' Jane asked.

'I don't think ＿＿,' Mrs Coe said. 'Her nose is cold and damp. ＿＿ just restless.'

'It's almost ＿＿ if she knows something is ＿＿ to happen.' They went to ＿＿ soon after.

A few hours ＿＿ they were woken by the ＿＿ thunderstorm Jane had ever known. The ＿＿ fell in torrents for ＿＿ an hour. Lassie hated it.

When it ＿＿ passed, they returned to bed. They all fell ＿＿ a peaceful sleep, including Lassie!

Now answer these questions in sentences:

1. How is Lassie's behaviour different from normal?
2. Why does Jane think Lassie might be ill?
3. Why doesn't Mrs Coe think Lassie is ill?
4. Why do you think Lassie hated the thunderstorm?
5. Why does everyone sleep peacefully after the storm?
6. Why do you think Lassie behaved as she did?

Traffic Gifts

Hazel and I were doing a jigsaw. I could ___ the noise of the traffic in the background.

'___ it always as noisy as this?' I ___ my cousin.

'As noisy as what?' ___ said. 'Oh yes, I suppose so. We ___ notice any more.'

I wondered how ___ it would take me to get ___ to it. As we worked on the ___, I heard a screech of ___.

'Someone's taken the corner too fast. ___ happens all the time. We'll ___ and look in the garden later.'

I wondered what ___. Later I found out. In the ___ was a hub cap. Hazel said, 'It's a pity it's ___ something useful. We get fruit and vegetables sometimes! We've ___ bags and cases. The best was a guitar in ___ case. It was never claimed. It's mine ___.'

Now answer these questions in sentences:

1. Where is the house built and how do you know?
2. What do the family think of the noise?
3. Why do you think the cousin is in the house?
4. What does the screech of tyres mean?
5. Where do you think the fruit and vegetables came from?
6. How do you think the guitar came to be in the garden?

Wild Cat

Sandra and Trevor looked in the book.

'There!' said Sandra, 'The prints ____ just like that!'

'I think you're ____,' said Trevor. 'It was a cat! But ____ one was it?'

'It has to be ____ one,' said Sandra. 'The mountain lion.'

'No one ____ believe us,' Trevor said. 'You ____ get them round here!'

____ was right. No one did ____ them. That was until the sheep was ____ dead, with the flesh stripped off.

____ came more reports of dead and mauled animals. One farmer ____ he too had seen the lion. He ____ it was a wild cat.

Experts ____ the zoo were called in ____ some fresh tracks were ____.

A police spokesman said, 'People are advised to ____ away from the area ____ this wild animal is ____ large.'

Now answer these questions in sentences:

1. Why do you think Sandra and Trevor were looking in a book?
2. What sort of book do you think it was?
3. What animal's prints have Trevor and Sandra seen?
4. Why does Trevor think no one will believe them?
5. Why were experts from the zoo called in?
6. Why did the police advise people to keep away?

Off the Lead

When Donna got home from school her first job ____ to take Mitzi out. Often ____ mother asked her to go to the ____ as well. Today she had been ____ for some milk. Andrew thought he ____ come too. He needed a ____ pen.

Andrew and Donna let ____ off the lead. She was a well ____ dog. Donna felt she could trust her.

____ went into the Post Office. Donna and Mitzi ____ over to the grocer's. Donna clipped on the ____ and tied Mitzi up.

When she came ____ of the shop, she took off the lead. Andrew ____ on the opposite pavement. He ____ over to them. Mitzi heard his voice. She ____ into the road towards him.

There was a screech of ____, and a car swerved.

They were all lucky ____ time.

Now answer these questions in sentences:

1. Why do you think Donna's first job is to take Mitzi out?
2. What can you tell about Mitzi?
3. Why did Donna tie Mitzi up?
4. Why did Mitzi run into the road?
5. Why do you think Donna didn't call Mitzi back?
6. What do you think happened at the end?

Harvest Time for Rabbits

'Look!' Sara said. Vicky looked. She ____ at the huge combine harvester. She watched it ____ and come towards them. It ____ to the end of the barley, stopped and turned, ____ went up the side. It ____, turned, and drove away ____ them. Vicky looked at the small square of ____ left in the middle of the ____. She looked at the combine working ____ the edges. She looked at the men ____ round. They were waiting for the ____ to finish.

Then she saw that ____ had a gun. As she watched, a rabbit ____ from the uncut barley. A hare followed. ____ they ran across the stubble there was a ____. Only the hare ran on.

'Why?' she ____. Then she knew. Rabbits and hares were ____. They did damage to crops.

Sara said, 'I wonder ____ many more are ____ in there?'

Now answer these questions in sentences:

1. What is the combine harvester doing?
2. Why do you think the combine works towards the middle of the field?
3. What happened to the rabbit?
4. Where are the small animals trapped?
5. What is their only chance of escape?
6. Why do farmers shoot rabbits and hares?

Laughter

'Look at me!' Colin called.

They all ____. He was standing on ____ of a wooden groyne. It was about one and a half metres ____. He was about to jump. Everyone ____ supposed to admire his skill. But ____ before the leap, he lost ____ balance. His feet seemed to fly ____ the air. His arms flailed. His head went ____ and he landed in the sand. ____ head stuck in, and his feet waved ____ in the air. He looked so ____ a cartoon character that Paula collapsed ____ laughter. Her parents ran to ____. They turned him the right ____ up. Paula carried on laughing.

'Is ____ all you can do, Paula?' her mother ____ crossly. Paula tried to stop. 'Colin ____ have broken his neck!'

Paula burst out ____ again. He had looked so funny ____ his head in the sand. She knew she ____ heartless. She couldn't help it. Her sides ached with ____. Her family was disgusted with ____.

Now answer these questions in sentences:

1. What did Colin mean to do?
2. What did Colin really do?
3. What did Paula find so funny?
4. How is Colin like a cartoon character?
5. Why were Paula's parents disgusted?
6. Why couldn't Paula stop laughing?

On the Beach

It was the fifth day of Stephen's holiday. He was cycling _____ youth hostel to youth hostel. This section of the _____ was along the coast. He _____ how nice it would be to _____ his lunch on the sand. He _____ some food at the shops. Then he _____ along the promenade. There was a clear _____ of sand by the sea wall. He carried his bike _____ the steps. Then he wheeled it _____ the beach.

After his _____, Stephen lay back. He closed his _____. Lulled by the sun and the _____ of the waves, he fell _____. In his dream his feet were bitten _____ an ice monster. The cold spread _____ his legs. He awoke with a start. The next _____ he was scrambling up the sea wall.

Now answer these questions in sentences:

1. What sort of holiday is Stephen having?
2. What time of year do you think it is?
3. Why did Stephen carry his bike down the steps?
4. Where did Stephen have his lunch?
5. Why did Stephen scramble up the sea wall?
6. Why do you think Stephen dreamed of an ice monster?

Horse Magic

'Would you like a ___ of tea?' my Mum asked.

'You never hear ___ horse magic now,' my Grandfather ___. He was off remembering again.

'___ is horse magic?' I said.

My ___ looked at me. 'I feel sorry ___ you, lad. You'll never know the old ___.'

'That's not ___ fault,' I said. 'But you might tell ___ what this horse magic is!'

'You never ___ Bob Smith did you? He lived ___ Red House Farm. He could ___ it.'

'Could do what?' I ___.

'Control horses. It looked like magic, ___ I don't expect it was. I've seen ___ stop his horse with a word. Then he ___ make it stand absolutely still. He could ___ it, and it wouldn't move a muscle ___ he came back.'

Now answer these questions in sentences:

1. Why doesn't the Grandfather answer the Mother's question?
2. Why is the Grandfather sorry for the boy?
3. What can you tell about how Red House Farm used to be?
4. What do you think has happened to Bob Smith?
5. What had the Grandfather seen Bob Smith do?
6. Why did the Grandfather describe what he saw as horse magic?

Leaving

The cart was laden. The bullocks ＿＿ nervous, and ready to go. ＿＿ little sisters were crying. My mother ran ＿＿ of the house.

'He won't ＿＿!' she cried.

'He'll be killed ＿＿ he stays!' my father shouted. '＿＿ all will if we don't ＿＿ now!'

He left the bullocks and ran ＿＿ the house. A moment later he ＿＿, pulling the old man. He bundled ＿＿ on to the front of the cart. We started ＿＿ the mountain. The hot air was ＿＿ thick with ash we ＿＿ hardly see, let alone breathe.

We children plodded ＿＿ behind the cart for many hours. ＿＿ last, we reached the city. We ＿＿ thousands more like us who were ＿＿ from the volcano. We heard, then, of ＿＿ who had not got away in ＿＿.

Now answer these questions in sentences:

1. Why do you think the bullocks were nervous?
2. Why do you think the small children were crying?
3. Why do you think the old man didn't want to leave?
4. Who do you think the old man was?
5. How did the children travel?
6. What do you think had happened to those who hadn't got away?

The Miracle

'Can we swim?' asked Ben, looking at the beach.

'Yes, if it's safe,' ___ his uncle.

'I can't ___ any notices. Julie can swim half a mile,' Ben said.

'And Ben can ___ a mile,' Julie said. 'We've been ___ for years.'

Some time later Uncle Bill noticed ___ waving. Then he realised they were ___ trouble. He ran into the ___ and started to swim out. ___ was a strong swimmer. But how ___ he save them both?

A woman ran ___ to Aunty Joan. 'It's the current,' she ___ . 'They won't have the strength to ___ in.'

Like a miracle, a man ___ a surfboard appeared in the sea beside ___ Bill. He reached Ben, who ___ it. Uncle Bill reached Julie.

It seemed ages ___ they all reached the shore. Aunty Joan flung towels ___ the shaking children. She hugged ___ . Then she turned to thank the ___ with the surfboard. She looked up the ___ and down. She looked ___ the water. He had completely disappeared.

Now answer these questions in sentences:

1. Why does everyone think it is safe to swim?
2. Why are the children in trouble?
3. What choice does Uncle Bill think he might have to make?
4. What is the miracle?
5. How are both children saved?
6. How do you explain what happened to the man?

Rats

Rats are a threat to health. They ___ diseases which can kill humans. Rats ___ in cities and in the country. ___ the country they destroy ___. In towns and cities they scavenge ___ stored food. They steal from dustbins and rubbish tips. They ___ try to get into food ___ and warehouses. If they do, the ___ is spoiled. It could infect humans and ___ them ill.

In cities the ___ live in sewers and cellars of ___. A big city will have hundreds of thousands ___ rats. In some ___, wild cats keep the rats ___. People then have to ___ up with awful screeches ___ night.

In other places, birds of prey ___ down the rats. The ___ then is to stop people from killing the ___.

Now answer these questions in sentences:

1. What can rats do to humans?
2. Where do rats live?
3. What do rats eat?
4. What other creatures keep down the rats?
5. What causes the screeches people have to put up with at night?
6. Why should people be stopped from killing birds in some places?

Colours

Most people prefer a few special colours. You can ____ this in the clothes they ____. You can also see ____ in the colours in ____ homes.

Think of the effect of ____. Does red wake you ____ or send you to ____? What would it be like ____ plants and leaves were red? ____ a lot of blue in a room ____ you feel warm? What ____ are found most often in bedrooms?

____ the past, colours have been ____ for healing. Gemstones such as rubies, sapphires, emeralds and topaz ____ used. Red stones were worn ____ troubles with the blood. Yellow ____ were worn to help liver ____. Green stones were ____ for the eyes. Blue stones were used ____ a tonic. They were also ____ to guard against evil.

Now answer these questions in sentences:

1. How would you know what someone's favourite colour is?
2. How could colours be used for healing?
3. Why do you think red stones were used for blood troubles?
4. Why do you think green colours were used for the eyes?
5. What two effects were blue stones supposed to have?
6. Can you give examples of red, green, yellow and blue gemstones?

On the High Seas

The trading ship didn't have a chance. She ____ left the East Indies only a few days ____. Trade had been good, and ____ she was heavily laden ____ silks and spices. The English court ____ prepared to pay for such luxuries.

The pirate ____ was light and quick. Its sails ____ up the smallest breeze. It soon outran the ____ ship. The pirates tied on ____ ship, and swarmed aboard. The crew ____, but were quickly beaten.

The goods ____ soon transferred. The crew were ____ up and taken aboard the ____ ship. The trading vessel ____ scuttled, and sank.

Two days ____, the crew were rowed ____ a tiny deserted island. They were ____ one keg of water. The last ____ they heard were the roars of ____ as the pirate ship sailed ____.

Now answer these questions in sentences:

1. Where was the trading ship going?
2. What had the trading vessel been doing?
3. In what ways was the pirate ship better in the water than the trading ship?
4. What happened to the trading ship?
5. Why do you think the pirates attacked the trading ship?
6. How might the crew be saved?

The Mountain Climb

The party set off early ___ the mountain before the heat built up. The ___ part of the walk was ___ woods. That was pleasant, although the path ___ steep.

As they ___ above the tree line, clouds ___. A hundred metres ___ the top the rain pelted ___. There was no cover. No ___ had a raincoat. It ___ rained for weeks, and this morning had ___ no different. They all crouched ___ a rise in the hill. Still ___ were soaked to the skin.

Ten ___ later, the sun came out and ___ out. Once more the party started ___. By the time they ___ the top, their clothes ___ drying, and they were warm ___.

Now answer these questions in sentences:

1. Why did the party set off early?
2. Why do you think they found it pleasant walking through woods?
3. Why didn't they bring raincoats?
4. What effect would crouching behind a slight rise have?
5. How long did the rain last?
6. Why were their clothes dry at the top of the mountain?

Claystead's Favourite German

The Mayor greeted 'Claystead's Favourite German' last week. He ____ Herr Erich Baden of Bonn, West Germany. ____ is Herr Baden's first visit to Claystead ____ the war. Then, he ____ a young man in the German Air Force. ____ 19th March, 1943 he was ____ a scouting mission. Somehow he lost the ____ planes. His plane developed engine ____ and lost height. Herr Baden knew he ____ have to land quickly. One of the engines ____ into flames. It was going to be a ____ landing. He got ready to jump. Then, ____ Baden realised he was coming ____ on a village. Risking his ____ life he stayed in the plane. Only ____ it was clear of the buildings did he ____ out. He landed in the Claystead School yard. The ____ crashed in the field behind the school. Herr Baden ____ both legs.

Thanks to ____ brave action, no one in the village was ____ .

Now answer these questions in sentences:

1. When was Herr Baden flying over the village?
2. Where were the other planes?
3. What was Herr Baden doing, flying over the village?
4. Why did Herr Baden need to land quickly?
5. Why did Herr Baden wait before he jumped out of the plane?
6. What risk did Herr Baden take by staying in the plane?
7. Did Herr Baden suffer by staying in the plane?
8. Why do you think Herr Baden is called 'Claystead's Favourite German'?

The Goshawk

The man walked through the crowd with the ___ on his leather glove. It ___ on a funny hood which ___ its eyes. Round one leg was a ___ tied to a leather strap, and ___ was a bell on each leg. The trainer ___ the people it was a goshawk, a hunting bird.

___ took off the hood, then slipped the string ___ the jess. The hawk ___ on the fence and watched. The ___ walked about twenty metres and ___ swinging the lure. This was a ___ of raw meat on a long string. He ___ it round his head. The hawk swooped ___ it. As it was about to clutch ___, the trainer swung it away. The ___ rose into the air and ___ round in a circle again. This ___ the trainer let the hawk ___ it.

Now answer these questions in sentences:

1. Why do you think the man wore a leather glove?
2. Why didn't the bird fly away when it was taken through the crowd?
3. Why do you think the bird had bells on?
4. What do you think a jess is?
5. What sort of bird is a goshawk?
6. What is a lure?
7. Why do you think the string is long on the lure?
8. Why do you think the trainer didn't let the bird get the lure at first?

Shopping

It was Friday. Mrs Lacey was ____ her shopping for the weekend. ____ weekend was special. Her son and ____ family were making a rare visit ____ her.

Mrs Lacey was flustered. She hadn't ____ a meal for anyone else in a ____ time.

In the supermarket, Mrs Lacey ____ at all the shelves. They might ____ soup, she thought. She popped a ____ into her basket. She stopped ____ the cheese counter. She'd better ____ a little more than her usual ____ of Cheddar. So it went on.

____ Mrs Lacey got to the checkout ____, she was surprised at the amount of food in her ____. She was shocked at the ____ of money she had to pay. Worst of ____, she was distressed to find she hadn't ____ money in her purse.

Now answer these questions in sentences:

1. What was different about this shopping trip for Mrs Lacey?
2. Why was Mrs Lacey flustered?
3. What can you tell about Mr Lacey?
4. What can you tell about how Mrs Lacey usually lived?
5. Why is Mrs Lacey surprised at the amount of food in her basket?
6. Why does Mrs Lacey become distressed?
7. What will Mrs Lacey have to do now?
8. How could Mrs Lacey have stopped herself getting into this embarrassing situation?

The Miller

My father's cousin came to visit us ____ Holland. They hadn't met ____ many years.

She told us ____ her childhood in a windmill, and ____ hard it had been for ____ mother to manage after the war.

'____ happened to your father?' I ____.

'He was taken away, and he ____ came back,' she said.

'But ____?' I asked.

'I told ____ he was a miller. He was ____ out sending signals.'

'Did he ____ a radio?' I asked.

'No, he ____ the sails of the windmill! There ____ many people who didn't ____ being occupied by the Nazis. My father was ____ of them. He ____ the resistance movement ____ the only way he could. We all ____ to give up something in the ____ for freedom. My father gave his ____.'

Now answer these questions in sentences:

1. Which country had the lady come from?
2. Why had it been hard for the mother to manage after the war?
3. Why was the miller taken away?
4. What had happened to the miller?
5. Who do you think found out about the signals?
6. How did the miller send the signals?
7. What can you tell about the resistance movement?
8. What can you tell about the sort of man the miller was?

Clowning

The circus was ____ to town. David couldn't ____ to go. He liked the horses ____ lions, and he liked the high wire acts. But ____ loved the clowns.

Sometimes, when life ____ gloomy, he thought of running ____. He dreamt of going to ____ a circus. But David had some sense. He knew ____ a circus wouldn't want ____! Still, it didn't stop him ____ he'd been born into a ____ family.

Then, in the newspapers, he ____ Leo the clown's story. Leo hadn't ____ born into a circus family either! He had ____ to a clowning college. He'd ____ to juggle and walk ____ the wire. When he was good ____, he joined a real ____. Now he was famous.

This gave David an ____.

'If he can, ____ maybe I can!' he said ____ himself.

Now answer these questions in sentences:

1. What could David hardly wait for?
2. Why did David think of joining a circus when life seemed gloomy?
3. What act did David like best?
4. Why wouldn't a circus want David?
5. Why does he wish he'd been born into a circus family?
6. How had Leo learned to be a clown?
7. What had Leo done after he'd left college?
8. What idea does Leo's story give David?

Oil

Many plants and small animals ____ in lakes and seas. ____ they die, they sink ____ the bottom and get covered ____ mud. If this goes on ____ a long time, a very deep layer is formed. ____ time, this layer gets buried ____ rocks. The pressure of the ____ turns the remains of the ____ and animals into oil!

It ____ like this, millions of years ago. The ____ is trapped now between rocks, under the ground. We get it ____ by drilling. This is done at sea, ____ well as on land.

We ____ oil to make things go, ____ cars and planes. As ____ as energy it can give ____ heat. Other things which ____ used today are made ____ it. Among ____ are soaps, plastic, nylon and fertilisers.

Now answer these questions in sentences:

1. What happens to dead plants and animals in seas and lakes?
2. What is the deep layer at the bottom made from?
3. What does the layer get buried by?
4. What turns the remains of the plants and animals into oil?
5. When did the sea-creatures live, which are now oil?
6. Where is oil formed?
7. What is oil used for?
8. What can be made from oil?

The Chance

Jud had made up his mind. He was going. ____ was the one chance they had ____ breaking free of poverty. There would also be ____ less mouth to feed when he went. And ____ he returned? Jud was confident ____ luck would be changed.

He said ____ to his family. He didn't ____ it, but he was one of 100,000 men who ____ to California that year. Many others had ____ the newspaper reports of gold. They all ____ for the lucky strike.

Jud ____ a mule and walked. It took ____ 20 weeks. Then he headed north to the ____ flowing from the gold fields. ____ he staked his claim, by marking ____ a piece of land with stakes he first had to ____. The hard ____ of digging, then washing the soil in the ____, began.

Now answer these questions in sentences:

1. Where did Jud decide to go?
2. Why did Jud decide to go?
3. Why did so many people go to California that year?
4. How did Jud carry his baggage there?
5. How did they know about the gold in California?
6. What is a lucky strike?
7. How did Jud stake a claim?
8. Why do you think the soil is washed in the river?

The Lucky Stone

Chris wondered if it would work. Darren _____ it had worked for him. He did _____ a BMX bike to prove _____!

The last time he had _____ his parents if he could camp out, _____ had refused.

He gripped the Lucky Stone _____ his pocket as he asked the question. _____ parents looked doubtful.

'Well,' said his _____, 'I'll phone your friend's father and _____ what he thinks.'

He went to the _____. The stone _____ to burn in Chris's hand. When his father came _____, he said, 'Yes, just _____ tonight. Then we'll see!'

As he went to _____ his things ready, Chris kept thinking, 'It _____! It really works!'

Now answer these questions in sentences:

1. How did Darren know the Lucky Stone had worked for him?
2. Why did Chris want the Lucky Stone?
3. What question do you think Chris asked?
4. Why does Chris grip the Lucky Stone when he asks his question?
5. What doubts do you think his parents might have?
6. Why do you think Chris's father phoned the friend's father?
7. Why do you think Chris's father agreed this time?
8. Do you think Chris is right in thinking the Lucky Stone works?

Oil Rig Worker

Uncle Harry came to visit. My Mum and Dad ____ he was well off. They said it was ____ he wasn't married. They also said it ____ because he was an Oil Rig Worker.

I ____ this job might suit me. I asked Uncle Harry ____ it. He told me he ____ twelve hour shifts. After his ____ is over, he eats, then ____ television. Sometimes he ____ snooker or cards. As he's a hundred miles ____ land, he can't go anywhere! But he ____ spends two weeks at a time ____ the oil rig. Then he flies back ____ two weeks' holiday. He is ____ engineer. He works in the drilling crew. He ____ it is hard, dirty work. Other ____ on the rig are technicians, drillers, radio operators, cooks and cleaners.

I am ____ about it!

Now answer these questions in sentences:

1. What do the parents mean when they say Uncle Harry is well off?
2. Where is the oil rig?
3. Why doesn't Uncle Harry go to a disco when his shift is over?
4. Why doesn't Uncle Harry go for a long walk when his shift is over?
5. What does Uncle Harry do when his shift is over?
6. If Uncle Harry sleeps for seven hours, how much free time does he get in a day?
7. What would you like most about Uncle Harry's job?
8. What would you dislike most about Uncle Harry's job?

The Glass Workshop

Sheila admired the lovely glasses in the showroom. She ____ their shapes and their colours.

____ the workshop, she had stood and ____ similar ones being made. The glassblowers ____ it all seem easy! She had watched them ____ a blob of molten glass on a long ____ of iron. She had seen ____ blow it and roll it and shape it. ____ had seen the coloured glass melted into ____. She had seen the ____ change colour as it was reheated. She had seen ____ finished piece cracked off the iron ____ the end. Yet she had been ____ that the molten glass couldn't ____ weighed or measured. It couldn't be touched ____ it was so hot, and it ran ____ thick syrup. Yet these glassblowers were ____ skilled they could turn this runny stuff ____ lovely objects, and even ____ whole sets to match!

Now answer these questions in sentences:

1. What is going on in the workshop?
2. What does each glass start as?
3. What happens to the colour of glass as it is heated?
4. Why do you think the molten glass couldn't be weighed?
5. What would happen if you touched the molten glass?
6. How is the finished glass taken off the iron?
7. What does Sheila see being made?
8. What do you think Sheila finds most amazing about the work of the glassblowers?

The Mountain in Winter

The icy wind hurled snow, like gravel, ____ our faces. Sudden gusts of wind kept ____ us off our feet. We knew ____ were on the right part ____ the mountain. It was just a case of ____ the gap down!

We could only see a ____ metres at first. Then the snow ____ worse and we were in a white-out. We ____ the compass to take bearings. We ____ there was a precipice close by, but ____ close? Susan started throwing snowballs in front ____ we walked. We focused on them. ____ one disappeared from sight, we knew ____ the edge was! From there we could ____ the gap, and our way down. Later, we ____ up to the precipice we nearly ____ off. It would have been a long ____!

It was a great day, we ____ later. But were we good ____ to climb the Alps yet?

Now answer these questions in sentences:

1. Where are these people?
2. What can you tell about the wind?
3. Why did the snow feel like gravel?
4. What is a white-out?
5. Why was a compass needed?
6. Why did Susan throw snowballs?
7. Why do you think these people are on the mountain?
8. What do you think these people are aiming to do?

Anting

Many birds can be seen anting. This is ＿ a bird picks up an ant in its ＿, and rubs it ＿ its feathers. Or it allows many ＿ to run through its plumage. ＿ a long time no one knew ＿ birds did this. Then it was ＿ that ants give off something ＿ formic acid. This is a substance ＿ other insects, like mites and lice, ＿ like! It is thought that ＿ go anting to keep themselves clean.

Now something ＿ has been found out about some ants. They ＿ give off an antibiotic. This ＿ kill the spores, which are like tiny seeds, ＿ some germs! Perhaps the birds are ＿ themselves healthy as well ＿ clean! But do you think they ＿ why they do it?

Now answer these questions in sentences:

1. What is anting?
2. What does the ant do when the bird picks it up?
3. Why don't mites and lice like being where ants have been?
4. What is formic acid?
5. What does an antibiotic do?
6. Where does this antibiotic the bird uses come from?
7. What can germs do to living creatures?
8. Why do you think birds go anting?

The Rock Concert

The doors opened, and Richard and Jonathan were ____ to get quite close ____ the stage. It was the first live rock ____ they had been to. Excitement built ____ as the hall became packed. Then the music started.

Jonathan ____ sure he wouldn't last till the second ____! He was so hot. Once, he ____ his hands above his head ____ cheer. It was so crowded he couldn't get ____ down for ten minutes! When Richard ____ to get a better view, the ____ surged. He couldn't manage to ____ his feet back on the ground ____ the crowd moved again. One fan climbed ____ to the stage. He was thrown back ____ the crowd. He had to crawl on his ____ and knees, on people's heads and ____, to the side before he could get ____ .

Now answer these questions in sentences:

1. Why do you think Richard and Jonathan were able to get near the front?
2. Why do you think they wanted to be near the front?
3. What is meant by Jonathan feeling he couldn't last?
4. Why do you think Jonathan is so hot?
5. Why couldn't Jonathan get his hands down?
6. What did Richard have to wait for?
7. Why did the fan have to crawl to the side?
8. Imagine you were Richard and Jonathan. What words would you use to describe the evening?

Nine Shillings a Day

'When I started in the pit, miners like us ____ for nine shillings a day. It ____ much more than the dole, ____ it was a job. Before the war, ____ weren't many of them.' The old ____ stopped.

'Living on nine shillings a ____ must have been bad. Wasn't it worse ____ you could die for that amount?' ____ Tom.

'Like those over ____ Gresford, you mean? Two hundred and sixty-five men dying ____ one disaster! They had to seal ____ the shafts, the underground fire was so ____. They left the bodies ____. It started because of the fire damp. Gas levels ____ built up, until the mine exploded. Everyone knew something was ____ to happen. Risks were ____ all the time, in order to ____ coal production up. We'd have ____ our jobs otherwise,' explained the ____ man.

'Instead, 265 men lost their ____!' replied Tom.

Now answer these questions in sentences:

1. What were there not many of before the war?
2. Why did the old man reckon work was better than the dole?
3. Why couldn't they save the men at Gresford?
4. What had caused the explosion at Gresford?
5. Why were the bodies left down Gresford colliery?
6. Why did everyone expect something to happen?
7. Why did the miners take risks?
8. What would have happened if less coal had been produced?

My Mother

My mother is odd. She is especially odd ____ the garden. If you want to tell ____ something, you won't find her in the kitchen ____ other mothers. She doesn't even watch television, ____ it's *Gardeners' World!* You've got to hunt outside ____ her. Then you share her attention ____ the plant lice. And you end up holding ____, or running round after her. It's up and ____ the garden for the hoe, ____ the twine, or something.

People have ____ up phoning her in daylight. And ____ my little brother wakes up, it's less bother to ____ to him than call her in. By the ____ she's got her wellies off and ____ her hands, he's either ripped up my homework or ____ back to sleep. Her fingers are stained ____ gardening. I'm ashamed on Parents' Evenings. She only ____ to the ones in winter.

Now answer these questions in sentences:

1. Where does the writer think most mothers are to be found?
2. Which is the mother's favourite television programme?
3. Why does the writer have to share the mother's attention with the plant lice?
4. What other disadvantages are there about going out in the garden?
5. Why doesn't the mother receive telephone calls in daylight?
6. Why is it simpler for the writer to do the babysitting?
7. Why is the writer ashamed of the mother?
8. Why does the mother only go to Parents' Evenings in the winter?

Windfalls

Did you know there are many reports ____ strange things falling ____ of the sky? The most common of ____ are frogs and fish. ____ have been known to ____ out of the sky alive!

It is hard to ____ but it is really true. Some people ____ to explain it by saying the frogs ____ have popped up from the ____. That doesn't explain how they were ____ on top of people's umbrellas!

____ seems to have happened is ____ a freak wind lifted these creatures ____ the air. If a tornado passes ____ water, it will suck up the water and ____ there is in it. It becomes a waterspout. The ____ spirals upwards. Then, maybe a few miles ____, frogs and fish are rained down! The ____ rained on get quite a ____!

Now answer these questions in sentences:

1. What does the passage say is hard to believe, and why?
2. What are the most common things to fall from the sky?
3. What can you tell from the fact they are still alive?
4. Do you think the water comes down with the frogs?
5. Why couldn't the frogs have popped out of the ground?
6. What is a waterspout?
7. What goes up with the water?
8. Why do the creatures land in another place?
9. How do the frogs and fish get from one place to another?
10. What can you tell about a tornado from this passage?

The Little Cat

The little cat was exhausted. All ＿＿ wanted was somewhere warm, somewhere ＿＿ food, somewhere she could stay. She ＿＿ her way through the cold wet bushes. There ＿＿ a hiss, and the little ＿＿ stopped. She cowered with fear. ＿＿ a cave of dry grass, formed ＿＿ a fallen fence post, ＿＿ a magnificent Tom cat. He looked, sniffed, ＿＿ leapt away through the undergrowth. She ＿＿ at a distance. He led ＿＿ to a door, outside which was a ＿＿ of milk and some scraps ＿＿ food. He drank, ate, then moved ＿＿. She crept up and finished the ＿＿.

The door opened. In a flash, the ＿＿ had disappeared. The little cat ＿＿ caught in the light. Two hands ＿＿ down, lifted her up, and ＿＿ her indoors. She couldn't understand the words, ＿＿ she knew that for a little ＿＿ at least she would be warm.

Now answer these questions in sentences:

1. Why do you think the little cat was exhausted?
2. What time of day is this?
3. What time of year is this?
4. Why does the Tom cat hiss?
5. Why does the little cat cower with fear?
6. How does the Tom manage to stay dry?
7. Why do you think the Tom led her to the house?
8. Why do you think there is food outside the house door?
9. Why did the Tom move away after he had eaten and drunk?
10. What do you think will happen to the little cat?

The Arrest

Dennis checked his speed. He had made good _____ since leaving the docks. It wouldn't do to be in _____ for speeding, on his first trip _____ a container lorry!

He glanced _____ the mirror again. A police _____ with flashing light and siren was in the distance, _____ towards him. For a moment, he _____ it must be after him! Then he realised it was _____ a grey car which was _____ down the middle of the road. Quickly, _____ the car had reached him, _____ swung the lorry _____ a tight turn. It jack-knifed, blocking the _____. The grey car screeched to a _____, and two men jumped _____. By this time the _____ car had pulled up, and _____ escape was blocked. Passers-by helped to capture them _____ jumping on one man. The _____ was held until police handcuffed both and _____ them away.

Now answer these questions in sentences:

1. Why did Dennis check his speed?
2. Where had Dennis collected his load?
3. What was on the lorry?
4. What is special about this day for Dennis?
5. Do the cars approach Dennis from in front or behind?
6. Why does the police car have the flashing light and siren on?
7. Why did Dennis jack-knife the lorry?
8. Why couldn't the men turn round and drive away?
9. How did passers-by help the police?
10. What will Dennis have to do now?

Mountain Rescue

Mountain Rescue teams save ____ who get into trouble ____ the mountains. Sometimes these are people ____ do not know how to behave on ____. Sometimes they are people ____ are skilled mountaineers, but who ____ an accident. On high mountains, the weather ____ change very quickly. It is easy to ____ lost in the snow and mist. If ____ are not prepared, and don't ____ what to do, you ____ suffer from exposure. This ____ when the wind and cold chill ____ body. Death can follow quite quickly.

Some teams abroad ____ German Shepherd dogs. Tests ____ shown that when a man was buried ____ 25 square metres of snow, it ____ 28 minutes for a man to find him. ____ took a man nine minutes ____ a metal dectector. It took a ____ half a minute. The test showed ____ a trained dog could speed ____ rescue work.

Now answer these questions in sentences:

1. What is a mountain rescue team for?
2. Why would the team be called out to rescue skilled climbers?
3. What might you do wrong if you did not know how to behave on mountains?
4. What is the danger from the weather on high mountains?
5. What is exposure?
6. Why is exposure dangerous?
7. Where are German Shepherd dogs used?
8. What is the slowest way to find a person buried in snow?
9. What is the quickest way of finding a person buried in snow?
10. Why is speed important in rescue work?

Science Fiction

Tex Batey liked to write ____ the future. He wrote Science Fiction stories. Each ____ he wrote a book, he had to ____ out a lot of facts. He talked ____ many scientists. He asked ____ what they were trying to find ____ at the time. He asked them ____ had just been discovered. He also ____ them what was likely to ____ next.

Tex thought some of the ____ to his last question were stranger ____ his stories! One scientist said work was ____ on to produce space ships ____ could travel at 19,000 miles ____ a second! This was likely to ____ achieved within the next hundred years. ____ this speed, the next star system ____ be explored. It would take 50 years to ____ there. Of course, crews would ____ be able to return to ____.

Now answer these questions in sentences:

1. What are Science Fiction stories?
2. Why did Tex have to find out a lot of facts before he could write his books?
3. Why do you think Tex has to find out these facts each time he writes a book?
4. Whom did Tex talk to when he needed help with his books?
5. What question did Tex ask about present work?
6. What question did Tex ask about future work?
7. What do scientists hope to explore in space in a hundred years?
8. Why will they have to wait 100 years?
9. Why do scientists need space ships to go as fast as 19,000 miles in a second?
10. Why wouldn't the space crew be able to return to earth?

The Old House

The dream was vivid. ____ detail was clear; the large ____, with the windows on three floors; the porch, ____ the round window above it. The gardens ____ down to the spot where Steve stood. ____ Steve awoke, the image of the house stayed with ____. He couldn't remember what ____ happened in his dream. All he could ____ was the house. The same ____ came to him a few more ____, then stopped as the years ____ by.

Later, when he ____ a soldier, Steve ____ in a detachment sent to guard some prisoners of war. ____ were stationed at an old hall, ____ they were to stay ____ the war ended. As they marched ____ the corner of the drive, Steve ____ up at the hall ____ the first time. It had ____ floors, and a round window ____ the porch.

Now answer these questions in sentences:

1. What part of the dream does Steve remember for some time?
2. What is unusual about the windows of this house?
3. How many flights of stairs must there have been, at least?
4. When do you think Steve stopped having the dream?
5. Is the house on a hill or in a valley?
6. Why do you think Steve became a soldier?
7. Where do you know Steve was posted for part of the war?
8. What was the detachment's job for the rest of the war?
9. Had Steve seen the old hall before?
10. What do you think you would feel, if you were Steve, when you first saw the house?

Forest Fire

When a forest burns, the burning wood ____ a noise like the crackling of dry ____. Birds ____ down the wind before the flames. Scared animals ____ to rush away from the spreading heat. ____ that fall are trampled down ____ others, or are overcome by smoke. ____ the flames reach fresh trees, there ____ bursts of hisses and crackles. The ____ smells strongly of burning wood, and sometimes also ____ fur and meat.

The animals ____ can escape, make for the river. ____ will tumble down the banks, or ____ themselves into the water. To cross the ____ to safety, they have to ____ against the current. They are ____ from the flames, but not ____ the sparks leaping from the burning bank, or the charred logs ____ fall into the river. Dead or exhausted ____ are carried helplessly downstream.

Now answer these questions in sentences:

1. What does the forest sound like when it's on fire?
2. Why do the birds fly before the flames?
3. What happens to the animals which fall?
4. Why does the smoke smell of fur and meat?
5. Why do the animals make for the river?
6. What do they have to do to get to safety?
7. What are the animals in the water safe from?
8. What are the animals in the water not safe from?
9. What can be seen in the river?
10. How will the forest be different after a fire?

Edith

Edith was an old lady ____ lived in a cottage quite ____ our house. She was considered to ____ quite mad, though harmless. She could often be ____ sitting in an old push-chair ____ the side of the road. She was ____ at dawn, winter and summer, and ____ often be heard shouting to someone ____ the time, or even for the day of the ____.

The strangest thing was her clothes. ____ was nearly eighty, and was bent double. She ____ huge, old men's boots, tied on ____ string. Round her legs she ____ newspaper and polythene. Her clothes appeared to be ____ up of layers of polythene sacks and newspapers, tied ____, and she clutched a blue polythene cloak.

People ____ her proper clothes, of course, but she burnt ____ or threw them out ____ the window. She was a strange ____.

Now answer these questions in sentences:

1. Why did people think Edith was mad?
2. Why do you think she used a push-chair?
3. What time did Edith get up in the summer?
4. How do you know she didn't wear a watch?
5. Why did she choose to wear newspaper?
6. Why did she choose to wear polythene?
7. Why was a polythene cloak sensible for her?
8. Why do you think people gave her clothes?
9. Why do you think she got rid of them?
10. Why do you think Edith is not put in an old people's home?

Flying

Christine often dreamed she flew through the streets, _____ the heads of people. She didn't _____ wings. She just moved her shoulders _____ a circle, from the front, up and over the back, _____ and under and up the front again. But as she _____ older, much more effort was needed, and she _____ fly as high. She had to tuck _____ her legs to avoid kicking _____ in the face.

One day she thought, I've never _____ it in real life! She was glad no one _____ see her, making the familiar movements. Her _____ were aching, when she felt a little jerk. Her _____ had left the floor. She worked _____. She was as _____ as the bed! She heard her brother outside and _____ to the ground, panting.

'What have you been _____?' he said.

'Nothing,' Christine replied.

Now answer these questions in sentences:

1. How did Christine travel in her dreams?
2. How did she move her shoulders?
3. What happened to the flying as she got older?
4. Why do you think Christine had never tried to fly before in real life?
5. Why do you think she was glad no one could see her?
6. Where was she trying to fly?
7. Why do you think she dropped to the ground when she heard her brother?
8. Why was she panting?
9. Why do you think Christine replied 'Nothing,' to her brother?
10. What would you do now if you were Christine?

Hijack

'This is Graham Waters. Here is a report ____ the hijack.' Graham kept glancing ____ the windows of the telephone box. The plane ____ still on the runway. When he had ____ the news through to his paper, he ____ back.

'What's happened?' he ____ another reporter.

'Still no agreement,' was the ____. 'The hijackers ____ release the passengers. The authorities won't ____ the prisoners asked for.'

Just then, they ____ a door open. Five figures ____ down the steps from the aircraft. Three ____ children.

'Any more?' Graham ____ an official.

'That's all,' he replied. 'The ____ 81 stay. If they ____ trouble, they'll be killed. One ____ one, the hijackers said, unless their demands ____ met.'

Graham could see food being loaded ____ to the plane. 'At least it ____ as if they are still talking,' he ____.

Now answer these questions in sentences:

1. What does Graham do at the airport?
2. What do you think his job is?
3. What do the hijackers want?
4. Why do you think the authorities are refusing the hijackers' demands?
5. What do the hijackers threaten if they don't get what they want?
6. Why do you think the children were released?
7. Why might you release some of the passengers if you were a hijacker?
8. Why do you think the authorities are letting them have food?
9. Why does Graham think the hijackers and authorities are still talking?
10. What would you do now if you were in authority?